Christ's Lane, 1885 (opposite) and c. 1910. The lane was stopped up in the 1960s when Bradwell's Court Shopping Centre was built.

CAMBRIDGE
THEN & NOW

Sidney Street, 1870 and 2002 (opposite). The urban landscape remains largely unchanged apart from the shopfronts and road surface. On the right is Sidney Sussex College, former college of Oliver Cromwell and last resting place of his head.

CAMBRIDGE
THEN & NOW

JOHN DURRANT

First published in the United Kingdom in 2002 by
Sutton Publishing Limited exclusively for
WHSmith, Greenbridge Road, Swindon SN3 3LD

British Library Cataloguing in Publication Data
A catalogue record for this book is available from the British Library.

ISBN 0-7509-3131-0

Illustrations

Front endpaper: St Andrew's Street, *c.* 1870.
Rear endpaper: St Andrew's Street, 2002.

DEDICATION

To the memory of my mother, Annie Emma Elizabeth Durrant, who died two days after I started to write this book.

Typeset in 11/14pt Photina and produced by Sutton Publishing Limited, Phoenix Mill, Thrupp, Stroud, Gloucestershire GL5 2BU. Printed and bound in England by J.H. Haynes & Co. Ltd, Sparkford.

King William IV public house, Newmarket Road, 1971. This was one of seventeen pubs and beerhouses between Christ Church and Barnwell Bridge. This historic hostelry, also known as the King Bill, had existed since at least 1839 and was demolished by 1977 to make way for the widening of Newmarket Road. This section of the road was once known as George IV Street.

Contents

Green Street, *c*. 1875 and 2002 (opposite). Formerly called Highe Warde Lane, it was renamed after the mathematician Oliver Green (1563–1623), who owned land between Sidney and Trinity Streets. A more colourful explanation for its title is that the street was closed up during a medieval plague and grass took it over.

Introduction

Cambridge Then & Now takes the reader on a journey back in time to sample the past and compare it with the present, to shed a tear over a vanished age, to applaud improvement or just to accept the inevitability of change. Some pictures will be very personal. The destruction of an historic building can be as painful as the loss of an old friend, a familiar landmark gone from an uncertain future. When we also view what has gone before us we feel robbed of our heritage and think that the perpetrators of such architectural crimes should be brought to justice. Demolition is, like capital punishment, irreversible. Nostalgia is not just a feeling about the past, for it drives decisions about our futures and influences how we judge what has been or is about to be done.

This collection of photographs offers the reader a chance to look through the time window from the Mayor's Parlour across the Market Square, to walk through the city centre and out along the Hills Road. After a look at Romsey Town we take a stroll along the Newmarket Road, then through the village suburbs of Cherry Hinton and Trumpington and on to Newnham Croft, ending at the Chesterton Road. Smell again

the 'rotten eggs' from the cement works against the backdrop of the black smoke of thousands of domestic fires. That is as much a part of old Cambridge as the soaring academic spires and the swish of oars upon the Cam.

As with *Cambridge Past & Present*, published in 2000, Tony Jedrej has walked in the footsteps of the old photographers. However, it was not always possible to replicate their pictures exactly. Not only are cameras different today, but also new buildings and flourishing trees obstruct sightlines, while traffic management has littered the townscape with signs, signs and still more signs. The quality of the old pictures remains high, not just because of the interesting subjects but through the skill of the early photographers. Most of these photographs are now conserved by the Cambridgeshire Collection.

As a child I wandered the town and wondered why 'they' were demolishing pleasant old buildings. I was not to know who 'they' were until years later when I was elected to the City Council and chaired both the property and planning committees. I found that I was but one of many, as a veritable host of people of various professions took, influenced or advised on decisions about what was saved and what was not. By then the development process could not be seen in such simple terms, of course.

Town planning in Britain was fairly minimal until the growth of statutory controls in the second half of the twentieth century. Much of what we admire about Cambridge is the product of land-owner decisions, i.e. the University and colleges. There was, however, no golden age before planning as even the great architects had to work with their patrons and sponsoring committees. The camel may be derided as a horse designed by committee – but in a desert what would you rather ride? What we currently view as the cohesion of the University was not the product of any single grand design. The colleges themselves often conceived impressive building schemes but failed to complete them. Even the most famous view of King's was only part of the original plan – with the chapel as one side of an uncompleted quadrangle. The earlier builders had their own problems of interrupted construction through civil wars, invasions and changes in monarchs, along with money

St Andrew's Street, 1898. From left to right, the Fountain, the police station, Spinning House and St Andrew's Street Baptist Church. The Spinning House was built as a workhouse in 1628 by Hobson's Charity. In the nineteenth century the inmates were mainly prostitutes imprisoned under an ancient privilege of the University. The vice-chancellor protected the morals of his students by imprisoning not only 'fallen women' but even lower-class women caught 'walking out' with undergraduates. The right was finally conceded to the civil authorities in 1894 after a famous court case, and it was the last legal power that the University held over the Town.

St Andrew's Street, 2002. Hobson House was built in 1901, replacing the redundant Spinning House with new police and fire stations. In the 1960s they moved to Parkside and were replaced by the City Council's housing department. The site remains in the ownership of the charity created by Thomas Hobson who, having made his fortune as a carrier and stable-keeper, still drove his own carts. His practice of only hiring out the freshest horse kept nearest the door gave the English language the phrase 'Hobson's Choice'. The Baptist Church was rebuilt in 1904 with a spire on its tower. Unfortunately this was deemed unsafe during the Second World War and removed. The Fountain moved to the other side of the neighbouring Llandaff House development.

shortages, religious strife and rivalry with their collegiate colleagues. If there is an overall theme to historic Cambridge, it is one based on chaos!

Good architecture is a balance between art and function; passion and emotion have as much validity in the process as reason. However, planning is driven by the guiding principle that development should be permitted providing it causes no demonstrable harm to interests of acknowledged importance. With innumerable influences upon a decision it is little wonder that the result may be the lowest common denominator, the building that does the least harm rather than the greatest good.

The urban landscape of Cambridge past would have had its own cultural atmosphere. What was in the mind's eye of those who saw the decaying river mills, the crumbling buildings replaced by new monuments like Foster's Bank, the hustle and bustle of the Victorian railway, the new University expansion, new churches, rural decline and creeping suburbs, ancient thatch replaced by brick and slate? How did people view

Abbey House, Abbey Road, *c.* 1905. This old farmhouse was built partly from reclaimed building materials from the defunct Barnwell Abbey in the sixteenth century and added to through the centuries. In 1946 Lord Fairhaven bought it as a new home for the Folk Museum to commemorate the salvation of the people of Cambridgeshire during the Second World War. Sadly the museum could not afford the conversion and eventually gave the building to the City Council. This year (2002) the council is considering its sale. Originally standing in virtual isolation in the pleasant and sleepy village of Barnwell, this property is now surrounded by housing and is close to one of the busiest junctions in the city.

'modern' architecture? Did they fear it or did they welcome it, did it inspire or depress them, or did they merely shrug their shoulders and ignore it as something in which they had no right to play a part? Contemporary society gives us all the right to play a part but we would fail if we decide simply on the basis of what we like. Of necessity architecture must from time to time stand apart from the crowd and lead us in new directions or else we will do more of the same and stagnate. Further complications arise when, through the benefit of our experiences in life, we change our minds. In a democratic age it is legitimate that we all have a view, what we love and what we hate, what we would save and what we would demolish, what should be built and what should be stopped. So whatever 'they' do will probably be wrong.

Indirectly, through our part in the consumer chain, we have all become 'they'. The demand for personal pensions has been so great that they became one of the largest sources of investment. They are often careful, risk averse and looking to the long-term, as we expect of them. Their choices were made in the market place in that they invested in new retail boxes and pulled down the old, quaint backward shops that we all liked but no longer patronised. Who are 'they'? 'They' are us!

Why is all of this so important? Cambridge is not just a beautiful place. Since the Middle Ages its primary function has been to host the University, which has become a world-class centre for education. Without the colleges Cambridge would be a small market town with an industrial base that would have been encouraged to fill the vacuum unoccupied by the academics. Once biblical Adam ate the apple from the proverbial tree of knowledge there was no turning back. Our survival depends on our ability to make beneficial alterations to our immediate and distant environment, to understand why the world is the way it is and how we might change it. The University is one of the keys to that global knowledge store. Cambridge is the future, which makes its past important to us all.

Market Hill to Hyde Park Corner

Market Day, 1870.

Market day, 1905. Traditional market days were Wednesdays and Saturdays but by the turn of the twentieth century a market was held daily with the main one on a Saturday. Contemporary stalls are now permanent and operate six days a week with a farmers' market on Sunday. Vehicle access is restricted during the daytime. The street scene has altered enormously with the construction of the white building for students from Gonville & Caius College with retail outlets at ground level. In addition, only the base now remains of the Victorian fountain, largely hidden from view.

Trinity Street and Green Street, 1878. For many years this corner was occupied by Whim Tea Rooms and Restaurant, much loved by town and gown alike. In the 1920s it was run by the Misses Walliker and up to the 1970s by Mrs Robinson and Miss Thornber. The current occupants are Hobbs but they were preceded by Laura Ashley, who moved to Foster's former bank. In the 1870s the site housed the printers office which produced the *Cambridge Express*. The current building was designed to include the solicitor's office of one of the Foster family and over the door is a family motto. For many years the author passed upon the stairs a window through which could be seen the inscription 'Fosters Wall', probably the last vestige of an old property dispute. Given the current narrowness of Green Street it is hard to believe that it was actually widened in 1878 by around 5 feet.

Foster's Bank, *c.* 1875, Trinity Street 1898 and 2002. Banks are everywhere! To the right in the middle and bottom pictures is the National Provincial Bank built in 1905 by Caroe and described by Pevsner as a pretty Art Nouveau corner house. In 1835 Foster's Bank moved from its first premises in Bridge Street to the timber-framed and pargeted building which was constructed in about 1600. Security measures included bank employees keeping watch at night. It remained in use until Foster's new building was erected in Sidney Street in 1890. For some time afterwards it was Matthew's restaurant and café and later the Turk's Head. Laura Ashley now occupies the site and the shop has been extended back into the converted banking hall in Green Street. Thurlbourn & Son (top picture) were tailors and robe-makers. On the corner of Green Street the old bookseller Deighton & Bell survives. During the nineteenth century Trinity Street provided financial and retail services not only for the town but also for growing numbers of well-heeled academics. Emphasis is now on tourists who flock to view the academic splendours of Cambridge.

St John's Street, *c.* 1875, and the former Selwyn Divinity School, 2002. The building above was formerly St John's College bakery and pensionary, a house for students for whom no accommodation was available in college. It was demolished in 1878 to make way for the Divinity School designed by Chamneys. The School has since removed to an innovative building in West Cambridge and this remarkable edifice is empty and awaiting transformation by St John's. All Saints' Passage borders the former church and yard of the same name demolished in 1864. Litchfield House to the right, with its distinctive frontage, is now the home of the Cambridge Music Shop but it once contained the All Saints' Varsity Toilet Club.

St John's Chapel, *c.* 1885. Completed in 1869 by Sir George Gilbert Scott, this striking building replaced an earlier chapel next door, of which only the foundations remain. Some original stone features were, however, salvaged. The woodwork for the new chapel was by the local firm Rattee & Kett. The construction of the new chapel brought about the closure of St John's Back Lane in 1862. Further clearances of town properties were made when St John's completed the construction right through to Bridge Street with Chapel Court in 1939. Despite the serious nature of college religious enterprises humour did surface from time to time. One master requested that he be buried by the chapel door so that the fellows could walk over him in death as they did in life.

The Hoop Inn, Bridge Street, 1820, 1870 and 2002. The Hoop was
built in 1729 and incorporated a private theatre because the
University banned public plays to protect the morals of its students.
The window lintels display thespian masks. In 1830 the hotel housed
the Shakespeare Club and three years later the Garrick. At the rear
the Amateur Dramatic Club still remains though the hotel closed in
1910. At one time four coaches per day left the Hoop for London,
and others went to Birmingham, Stamford, Bury and Huntingdon.
This is the only remaining narrow section of Bridge Street,
reminiscent of the once tight street plan of the town, altered through
the centuries by continued college expansion and later corporation
road widening to cater for a burgeoning number of cars.

Jesus Lane, *c.* 1900. It used to be known as Nun's Lane after the Benedictine Nunnery of St Rhadegond which was appropriated for Jesus College. At the junction with Park Street can be seen three houses that were later demolished for road widening. On the other corner was the Society of Friends' (or Quakers') meeting house, let as a public library until the latter found a new home in the Guildhall in 1862. The house was rebuilt in 1969. The Royston Arms operated from the 1870s through to the 1920s. After suffering bomb damage in the Second World War the wall on the right was rebuilt further back to widen the road. In the distance is the range of buildings that became the headquarters and garage of Marshall of Cambridge in 1912.

Green Street, 1910. This was once a cul-de-sac for vehicular traffic. It was widened to its current size in 1819. At the turn of the nineteenth century much of the street contained apartments and residential properties with only a small number of retail outlets. Herbert Robinson Ltd, now part of the Co-op, occupied the garage in the 1920s. Above next door was the former Wesleyan chapel that was vacated when the new church was built in Hobson Street in 1850. The University Debating Chamber took over until it moved to new premises in Bridge Street, and it was followed by the Theosophical Society. Eaden Lilly's, the well-known Cambridge department store, expanded back from its frontage in Market Street into Green Street. The store has recently closed and the premises have been sold to Borders. Shopping at street level has continued to grow and in 1999 the council repaved the roadway to promote city centre retail. Sidney Sussex College can be seen at the end of the street.

Sidney Street, *c.* 1925. It used to be called Conduit Street after the pipe that brought water from Conduit Head Road via Trinity to the tap on the wall of the Grey Friars, now Sidney Sussex College. By 1904 G.P. Hawkins had opened his Dorothy Café and Restaurant at 20–21 Sidney Street, extending into no. 22 in 1919 and nos 23–24 in 1930. By 1933 he also had a chain of seven bakery and confectionery shops. In 1948 the Dorothy Café was rebuilt with the current façade and the building still contains a number of original internal features. It had its own sprung ballroom floor and was a popular meeting place and entertainment venue for generations until closure in 1972. It is now occupied by Waterstones.

The Central Cinema, Hobson Street *c.* 1929, *c.* 1930 and 2002. Hobson Street was named after Thomas Hobson, the famous carrier. It was formerly called Walls Lane as it was part of the town's somewhat weak defensive system. The Central Cinema was opened in 1921 in the converted garage of the Cambridge Automobile & Engineering Company. It was rebuilt in 1930 but closed in 1972 when bingo replaced films. Many local children will remember the popular Saturday morning matinées. Little has changed on the frontage except for the canopy and the disappearance of the advertisement on the roof.

Sidney Street, 1944. The street once contained many local family firms, including the coachbuilders Hunneybun, established in 1727. The advent of national retailers with huge economies of scale, such as Woolworth's, Boots and Marks & Spencer, has changed the character of all city centres. F.W. Woolworth's bazaar made it to Cambridge by 1933 and advertised 'nothing over sixpence'. M&S expanded both ways into the premises of Miller's Music and the well-remembered Coad's. The concrete structure in the roadway was a wartime water tank for dousing fires.

Sidney Street, 1922. Boots the Chemist first arrived in Cambridge in the 1890s with a shop on Market Hill. By 1898 the firm had moved to Petty Cury and begun the process of extending the premises, culminating in the major expansion through into Sidney Street that began in 1929. A new building line was established to cater for the increasing traffic.

Sidney Street and Hobson Street, *c.* 1885. The corner property was a private house until it was converted into a shop with offices above before the turn of the century. In 1891 Banham & Benton, tailors, leased the site with the next-door shop and sub-let the offices above to the Ocean Accident & Guarantee Corporation. In 1890 Foster's opened its magnificent bank, which was one of only eighteen note-issuing private banks. It merged into the Capital & County Bank in 1905, which in turn became Lloyds in 1919. Sixteen years later the bank bought the freehold from the council and demolished the corner site to rebuild in a similar external style to Foster's premises. This is the site of the medieval Barnwell Gate and the contemporary closure prohibiting daytime traffic is its modern successor, keeping out cars rather than invaders.

Downing Street, *c.* 1950. First based in Regent Street with twenty-four lock-up garages in Canterbury Street, Camtax later moved into the former fire station occupied by Bowman's Garage in Downing Street. Camtax was the first taxi company in the country to install radios; the development came in 1946, with equipment supplied by Pye Telecommunications. In the distance is the distinctive St Columba's Presbyterian Church, built in 1891. The modest sign on one of the smaller properties was soon to be replaced when estate agents January's rebuilt their offices. The whole site is now occupied by the Rat & Parrot.

St Andrew's Street and Downing Street, 1938. The Cambridge Building Society was formed in 1850 after a meeting at the Guildhall chaired by the mayor. The aim was to make 'every man his own landlord'. The Society's first offices were in Post Office Terrace until the Lion Yard redevelopment. In 1967 it moved to St Andrew's Street after purchasing the G.P. Hawkins tea-room and Mac Fisheries shop from the Co-op. The corner shop was later purchased from the council together with the Royal Insurance Company premises in Downing Street. With site assembly complete, the premises were refurbished in 1996. Much house building in the twentieth century was funded by building societies, without which today's urban landscape would have been very different.

The New Theatre and the offices of the *Cambridge Daily News*, 1929 and 1948; Janus House, 2002. The Theatre Royal opened in 1882 in a disused skating rink. After this success the popular New Theatre opened in 1896, led by W.B. Redfarn, local artist and four times mayor. Despite some experiments with risqué revues the postwar period was too difficult and the theatre closed in 1956. (It was still called 'new' when it closed!) January's saw it as a prime site for offices and built Janus House here, named after the two-faced god. The *Cambridge Daily News*, founded in 1888, is the sole survivor of a number of Cambridge publications, having bought out its established rivals like the *Chronicle*, the *Independent Press* and the *Express*. It moved to Newmarket Road in 1962 but by 1994 it had moved again, this time to Milton, outside the city.

Camden Place, Regent Street, *c.* 1935. Named after Camden House in Park Parade, this terrace of fine town houses was built in 1881. They were first occupied as family housing although one did hold a preparatory school for young gentlemen. As elsewhere, institutional uses began to take over, particularly after the First World War, such as the University Arms annex, the County Council dispensary, and a painful extractor of teeth alongside a painful extractor of money – a dental surgeon and the Inland Revenue! By 1938 all the houses, apart from the tax office, were vacant and awaiting demolition. The war may have interrupted the process but by 1948 the Post Office had built the new telephone exchange, Telephone House. With changes in telephony BT moved out and the building has since undergone refurbishment for the University Local Examination Syndicate. The redevelopment included creating a feature entrance on the side and stopping up the front door.

The University Arms Hotel, Regent Street, *c.* 1905. The frontage was the earliest part of the hotel, built in 1834. It became one of Cambridge's top hotels when it was redeveloped by the Bradford family. In the 1960s the original façade of the hotel was replaced with the current frontage. Controversy raged over a proposal to build a car park for the hotel under Parker's Piece but this scheme was never achieved. Next door to the hotel, in what is now Pizza Hut, was the pianoforte dealership of H. Leavis, father of critic F.R. Leavis.

Regent Street, *c.* 1915. This photograph was used on a Christmas card. The run of premises included the Glengarry Hotel, now the Regent, the Ryecroft Rubber Company selling waterproofs and the People's Boot and Shoe Stores. This was the first home of Newnham College for women when it was established in Cambridge in 1871. Conditions were cramped and the ladies had no recreational space and could only look enviously at the sports activities on Parker's Piece. The college soon moved to Merton Hall in Northampton Street. Regent Street developed when the station opened in 1845 and more and more people travelled in this direction. Some properties were originally built as houses but were soon converted into shops and commercial premises. Note the sign for the emigre watchmaker, (Otto) Wehrle, whose brother traded in Sidney Street (*see* p. 6).

Along the Hills Road & then to Romsey Town

The Hills Road area, 1954. Note the amount of land then devoted to railway yards and sidings, since redeveloped for other uses. The Cattle Market, opened in 1885, was once an extensive operation with a number of auctioneers and its own bank branch. The farm site now houses the Clifton Road industrial estate. A large entertainment complex is currently under construction on the redundant market site. It includes a multi-screen cinema, although in 1936 the Borough Council decided that the site was unsuitable for such a use!

Hyde Park Corner, Regent Street, 1965. The origin of the name is obscure but probably mimics London as it is situated at the end of Regent Street. Given the volume of traffic at this junction it would be hard to imagine an Esso garage on this site today. Edward T. Saint was operating here in the 1920s and was followed by Herbert Robinson alongside Turner & Hore at the Hyde Park Garage. To the right was St Andrew's Terrace, which once contained W. Ison's cycle stores. He also had premises in Chesterton (*see* p. 121).

The Roman Catholic church from Parker's Piece, 1947. Cambridge is a city without a cathedral although the Church of Our Lady and English Martyrs, built by Rattee & Kett, is the next best thing. This junction was also the site of the important wayside Daws Cross. Gonville Place, on this side of the Piece, was named after the college because of its large land holdings in the area. The origin of Hills Road lies in the road to the Gogs at Wandlebury, named after the pagan gods Gog and Magog.

Hills Road, 1909, 1914 and 2002. The horse-drawn tramcar service was introduced in 1880 but withdrawn in 1914. Electrification had been mooted but the horses had objected. The building on the corner was the Great Northern Hotel. To the left offices have replaced the terraces of town houses next to the entrance to the Botanical Gardens. A tramcar similar to the double-decker illustrated was recently rescued from Ely where it had been used as a cobbler's workshop and garden shed. It is believed to be the sole survivor of the fleet that was sold at auction in 1914. It is in poor condition and awaits restoration.

Foster Mills, Station Road, *c.* 1925. The Foster family moved their milling operation to the station area alongside their coal yards in 1864 to utilise the growing railway network and the river mills consequently went into terminal decline. Known as Homepride Mills in the 1920s, it still sports the name Foster Mills despite its purchase by Paul Brothers in 1915 and Spillers in 1945. Electricity replaced steam and a new concrete silo was added in 1954. It remains one of the most prominent buildings in Cambridge, even more so than Kings College. With the decline of agricultural processing this mill may also become redundant and be converted for housing.

Station Road, 1922. This road once had a grand aspect, lined as it was by large houses set behind mature trees with a variety of comfortable names such as Salisbury, Anglesey, Woodstock, Richmond and Cleveland. Salisbury Villas survived on the east side, albeit turned over to institutional uses, but on the west side houses gave way to large office blocks named Daedelus, Demeter, Leda and Jupiter. One remnant of the former grand entrances remains next to Kett House in the form of an entrance pillar to the long-gone Clifton Villa.

Hills Road, *c.* 1925 and 2002, Poplar Cottage, *c.* 1950. The noted firm of James Rattee & George Kett was pre-dated by Catherine Rattee's similar business on Hills Road. James Rattee himself once lived in Poplar Cottage but he died in 1855. Rattee & Kett built their wood- and stone-carving works next door and the building works were on Purbeck Road. Kett House had replaced the works by 1962 and forty years later underwent a complete structural refurbishment. The artwork on the side of Kett House relates to George Kett's infamous ancestor Robert Kett, who led what became known as the Kett rebellion of 1381. It depicts Kett, a Norfolk farmer, holding a meeting under Kett's Oak. The family sold their connection with the firm in 1926. In 1381 Cambridge inhabitants actually sacked Corpus Christi College during the Peasants' Revolt but there is no memorial to the event!

Hills Road, 1909, 1913 and 2002. When James Berry Walford bought out his predecessor to start his own motor-bus company in 1907 the people of Cambridge were a little unreceptive as their previous experiences had not been good. One operator had been prosecuted because the bus 'failed to consume its own smoke'. However, Berry, who lived in Mayfield, persevered and was so successful that within seven years the tram company had closed down. The 'Ortona' name came from an Adriatic cruise ship. In 1931, with the onset of restrictive government legislation, the company was absorbed into the newly formed Eastern Counties. The depot, rebuilt in 1953, remained on Hills Road until the newly privatised Cambus moved to Cowley Road in 1987 and new offices were erected here for Mills & Reeve, solicitors

The Royal Albert Almshouses, Hills Road, 1859. Either the painter indulged in a little artisitic licence or this picture was subsequently changed, as it does not match what was built. The Mayor, Charles Balls JP, laid the foundation stone on the anniversary of Victoria's coronation. After a service at Great St Mary's civic dignitaries and friendly society members processed to the Hills Road site for the ceremony. The Royal Albert Benevolent Society for Decayed Tradesmen and Others had been fundraising since its creation in 1846. There were twenty-five occupants in 1922, only two of them male. All were referred to as inmates.

The LMS Depot, Hills Road, *c.* 1955, and City House, 2002. The LMS was one of five independent railway companies operating in Cambridge. Each company had its own goods station and cattle and coal wharves. The LMS depot was shared with E. Pordage, fruit wholesalers. City House was built in the late 1980s but has never been occupied to date because of a dispute with the builders. Reconstruction is at last taking place.

Hills Road and Cherry Hinton Road, c. 1935. Cambridgeshire Motors had a Ford franchise and were advertising the 250,000th Ford in Great Britain. Many of the early garages were situated in the town centre in converted buildings. However, as traffic increased, particularly in the postwar period, several dealerships closed or moved out on to the main roads. The Marshall Group now owns Tim Brinton's garage.

Cherry Hinton Road, 1922. This was once farmland in Cherry Hinton parish but it was taken into the town in 1912 when the boundary was extended to the vicinity of Mowbray and Perne Roads. St John's parish, previously known as West Cherry Hinton, was formally constituted in 1897, and the old parish became St Andrew's Ward. It was, however not long before St John's became part of Cambridge.

Cherry Hinton Road, 1925. With the growth of the new suburban developments such as the Rock estate and the Cavendish estate on Hills Road, this became an important local retail area. In 1898, when the British Electric Traction Company was proposing to take over the horse-trams, it suggested that the line should be extended along Cherry Hinton Road to the Rock Hotel. Nothing has come of it – yet!

Mill Road, *c.* 1905. The first St Philip's Church was a wooden building but by 1892 it had been replaced in brick and stone. It stands on the corner of Thoday Street, named after the local builder Herbert Thoday. His wife was commemorated in the adjacent Catharine Street at the other end of the terrace next to the church. Over the years this terrace has gradually been taken over by the Co-op, whose no. 1 Branch was at 177–179 Mill Road.

Mill Road, *c.* 1925. The growth of Romsey Town and Mill Road took off when the railway was crossed in the early 1880s and was largely based on railway and ancillary workers. The 'town' was named after Romsey Cottage, which was one of the few buildings in the area in 1846. Later this was the site of Romsey House. Residents today are probably relieved that it wasn't named after the other building nearby, Polecat Farm! Ground-floor shops were constructed over the years over the original gardens of the houses and can clearly be seen in the modern photograph.

Mill Road and the Lodge, *c.* 1925, and the Broadway, 2002. The Broadway, composed of fourteen shops with flats above, was built in 1936 and was given its own name to render unnecessary the renumbering of the whole street. The shops replaced the Lodge, which was set in its own grounds between Sedgewick Street and Cavendish Road. It was occupied by George Smith JP, a coal merchant and sometime Liberal councillor for Romsey. Some local people still claim to remember him and his generosity at his annual teas for young people.

The Earl of Beaconsfield, Mill Road, 1920. This public house on the corner of Great Eastern Street was named after the former Conservative prime minister, Benjamin Disraeli, who became the Earl of Beaconsfield. It reflected, along with the presence of the Salisbury Conservative Club, a strong Tory vote among the working classes. Change was to come in the 1920s when Romsey elected Labour councillors, built its own Labour club and earned itself the nickname Red Romsey or Russia. Note the small shop in the front garden, which was said to be open twenty-four hours to serve railway workers on night shift.

Mill Road Bridge, *c.* 1915. Cambridge did not expand beyond the railway until the early 1880s but within twenty years Romsey had developed into a small town. The bridge, which is such a feature of Mill Road, was not erected until 1889 when the level crossing and footbridge were replaced because vehicular traffic had become too heavy. Thereafter the area could truly be known as 'Over the Bridge'. In 1980 the bridge was rebuilt again and several houses and shops that pre-dated it, but looked on to it from their first-floor windows, were demolished. The footbridge was re-erected across the Cambridge–King's Lynn line on Stourbridge Common until electrification made it unsuitable. Thereafter British Rail donated it to the North Norfolk Railway at Holt. The corner shop on Cavendish Road was demolished for yet another road widening scheme. The houses that once stood on what is now the Great Eastern Street car park are also clearly visible next to the bridge in the picture above.

Cherry Hinton, from Uphall to Netherhall

Rectory Farm, *c.* 1895. Despite the mechanisation of farming there were still eleven people involved in the threshing process. At the turn of the twentieth century Cherry Hinton was an agricultural village but one hundred years later, like much of Cambridge, the agricultural element in the workforce had declined so much that it was barely visible in the urban landscape. Rectory Farm was also noted for the charm of its walnut tree avenue, but this did not save it from the onslaught of new housing which swamped the village.

The Norman Cement Works, 1954, and Lime Kiln Hill workings, 1951. Extraction for lime working was a traditional small-scale local industry but mechanisation transformed the landscape by gouging out vast tracts of the countryside. The Norman Works was the last (and the greatest) to be created, in 1904. Nearby on the same railway line was the Saxon Works, which had opened in 1901. By 1948 it had closed and had become a Territorial Army Centre. There was one other, the Romsey Town Cement and Lime Co., in Mill Road. The Atlas Artificial Stone Works stood on the site of J. Sainsbury's supermarket in Coldhams Lane. The Norman Works chimney belched out fumes and on a bad day permeated everywhere with the smell of 'bad eggs' and encrusted fences with dust. Some evidence of the workings remains in the overgrown pits on Lime Kiln Hill and in the two pits next to the Norman factory site. Others were used as landfill sites for domestic refuse. The factory site was cleared in 1988 and awaits imminent redevelopment.

St Andrew's Church, Cherry Hinton, 1845. Built in the Early English and Perpendicular styles and rebuilt in the 1880s, the church replaced a previous Norman structure. However, recent house building in nearby Rosemary Lane has revealed a previously unknown Saxon church and cemetery containing over six hundred burials. The current view of the church is largely obscured by trees and disfigured by traffic lights. Once called Hinton, the village had gained its current name by 1576 from the cherry trees. Only one now remains, in poor condition, in the Spinney. An alternative name could have been Saffron Hinton after the proliferation of saffron fields between the village and Cambridge. The village was created from two manors, Uphall on the high ground around the church and Netherhall down the High Street.

The village schools, *c*. 1915. On the right is the Church of England Infants' School built in 1818 by the Revd Bewick Bridge, mathematical scholar and vicar from 1816 to 1833. He was commemorated in a road composed of post-war prefabs but sadly the name was extinguished on the construction of the Teversham Drift estate. The school was rebuilt in the 1970s. On the left were the Five Bells and the Hopbine, two of the eight public houses that served a population of about 1,000 in 1891. Next door was Robert Cottage, possibly a former dame school, which was demolished to make way for the car park in 1966.

The railway crossing, *c.* 1915. The railway came to Cherry Hinton in 1845 with the opening of the Cambridge–Ipswich line. Sadly the station was one of the first closures in 1854. Early timetables show that the station continued to exist but no trains stopped there. In 1891 the village petitioned for reopening but to no avail. Controversy has raged in recent years with proposals for a new station being rejected on the grounds that it would attract too many cars. Village representatives had earlier campaigned for full barriers for the crossing when the rather quaint manual gates were replaced. The line is now single-track. In 1811 the sale particulars of the Red Lion mentioned the advantages likely to be conferred on the property by the imminent arrival of a canal but nothing came of this scheme.

High Street and Fisher Lane, *c.* 1905. Built in 1883, the Baptist Chapel had room for 300 'sittings'. Cherry Hinton was an 'open' village; there was no single resident landlord, so agricultural labourers and the like were free to worship at the place of their choosing rather than at the direction of their employer. The rival establishment in the terrace next door, the Russian Arms beerhouse, is somewhat oddly named given that the Russian Tsar was perceived as the major threat to the British Empire until 1904, when relations improved through the Entente Cordiale with France. The name persisted into the 1930s when the premises traded as a general dealer's under the name of the Russian House.

High Street, 1930. Cherry Hinton lost its independence and its parish council in 1934 when it was finally absorbed into Cambridge. Over the remainder of the twentieth century the village was to undergo a radical transformation with the construction of large housing estates off the High Street. Sadly neither landowners nor developers valued the ancient and Victorian properties that gave the village its character and the council of the times did little to defend them. As a result much has been lost, including some remarkable old thatched cottages. The photograph on the right illustrates what has survived, more by luck than design. The original structure has been extended and altered but nonetheless it still retains an element of its original character. For some years it served as a shop, but now houses a branch of Lloyds Bank. To the left runs the ancient footway Love Lane.

High Street, *c.* 1905, 1924 and 2002. The thatched cottage in the left foreground (in the middle and bottom pictures) was once a larger house but it has been converted into a florist's. The thatched house to the right was demolished to build a petrol station, which in turn was removed to create the shops and houses along Wedgewood Drive. In the distance can be seen the sign for the Chequers public house. The only traffic needing calming at the turn of the century were the sheep.

High Street, *c.* 1905. Only the terraced houses directly fronting the road remain. The Chequers was demolished in the 1960s and was eventually replaced by a housing development in the 1990s. Unfortunately, the row of thatched cottages known as Chequers Yard succumbed to fire. The recreation ground to the right was created from 4 acres of land after the First World War as the village memorial but went unmarked until the recent commemorative sign was erected.

Mansfield's, High Street, *c.* 1905. Henry Dickerson Mansfield was himself a noted local photographer and took this picture of his grocery shop and post office. A number of his prints were sold as postcards. He also made sausages. He wasn't running the post office in 1903, however, as it was listed to Charles Papworth, the wheelwright. For some years the Co-op ran the shop, which still contains the post office today. The site to the right is that of the Unicorn public house, which had yet to be extended.

High Street, *c.* 1915. Only part of this range of properties has survived redevelopment. 'Get Right With God' proclaims the sign over the gateway to Ebenezer Cottage, the home of Charles Scott, builder, painter and decorator, undertaker and lay preacher. The water pump on the right of the road served the steam lorries as they trundled between the chalk pits on Lime Kiln Hill and the cement works.

Robin Hood & Little John public house, 1915, 1953 and 2002. Once a small thatched cottage on the Fulbourn Road, it was extended at the beginning of the twentieth century and the gable-ended section was added by 1920. The whole site was then cleared and the current building erected. It has also been extended. In 1915 W. West drew the inn sign as 'The Little John & Robin Hood'. The signboard on the corner plot in the 1953 photograph bears witness to its proposed sale as land for housing. Local protests not only encouraged the council to purchase the area but also forestalled designs by planners to turn it into a safe recreation ground. It now has a secure future as the Spinney Nature Reserve. Nature does reclaim its own – this is a former industrial estate, hence the name Lime Kiln Close. On the opposite side of the road is Giant's Grave, the head of the spring upon which Cherry Hinton was founded.

The Red Lion, Mill End Road, 1930. The Red Lion is one of the village's oldest public houses and until recently sported an original insurance plaque from the eighteenth century. Many local hostelries were not listed by name in the trade directories as they were only beerhouses, unlike the Red Lion, the Unicorn and the Chequers. The historic clunch and brick wall was shortened to widen the frontage and in recent years the brewery has altered the character of the site by reducing the wall still further.

Mill End, *c.* 1915. This was one of the few side roads off the High Street until the twentieth century. It led to Sidney Farm and then by Daws Lane to the back of Cherry Hinton Hall. To the left is the former blacksmith's shop, rebuilt with a date stone in 1878. It provides an income for the Poor Estate, which includes the almshouses next door. The village feast was traditionally held in Mill End (also called Round Town) in the first week in October. The revived Cherry Hinton feast is now held on the recreation ground.

Mill End, *c.* 1924. When the author moved into one of the first new houses in this road in the 1960s it still had grass verges and gas lamps. Even the gas lamps had not yet been introduced in the 1920s. Despite the urbanisation of this old road it still contains one of the oldest properties in the village, Pegg's Yard at no. 84. The deeds for this date back to the 1700s.

Cherry Hinton Hall, *c.* 1970. John Okes built the Hall in 1839 in mock-Elizabethan style. It was sold in 1870 for £5,400. According to the sale particulars it included a miniature park, brick stabling, two full orchards and rich pasture totalling 35 acres in all. The most notable owner was William Phene Neal, later Lord Mayor of London. Cambridge City Council bought the hall from Trinity College in 1937 for use as a youth hostel, although part of the grounds went to Ridgeons, which became part of the Walpole Road estate. During the war the hall served as a fire brigade training depot; it later housed young evacuees from London and then became a nursery school. It is now the home of the Council's Employment Foundation Scheme. The park itself remains arguably the finest public open space in the city and annually hosts the internationally renowned Folk Festival.

Along the Newmarket Road

Watts' Brick and Timber Yard, Newmarket Road, *c.* 1875. The artist would have been in the vicinity of Coldham's Lane. To the right is the Cambridge–Ely railway leading under Barnwell Bridge in the distance. Only a short terrace of houses then stood on the Newmarket Road. The Leper Chapel can be seen close to the bridge.

King Street and Jesus Lane, 1878. Undergraduates had the 'King Street Run' where they competed to have a pint in every pub, but Newmarket Road was the real test. In 1906 Eglantyne Jebb, the great social reformer and founder of Save the Children, quoted that in one stretch of Newmarket Road there were twenty-two pubs in 796 yards – that's one pub every 36 yards! The Garrick or Garrick Head was demolished to make way for what may have been a Victorian road-widening scheme. The current junction of Maid's Causeway, Short Street, King Street, Jesus Lane and the relatively new Victoria Avenue is called Four Lamps.

The Zebra, Maids Causeway, *c.* 1925. Maid's Causeway was so named because the charitable Dr Perse is said to have bequeathed money in his will in 1615 to build a raised path for the two poor widows and four poor maidens of the Knights Almshouses to have a dry walkway above the flood line. The number of public houses had begun to decline after the First World War but the breweries saw value in an investment and rebuilt some to higher standards. The Zebra, on the corner of James Street, had existed as a beerhouse since at least 1867 and was rebuilt in the 1930s.

The Bird in Hand, Newmarket Road, *c.* 1905. It is situated in the heart of Barnwell, once a small village outside the town. Next door was the Priory Brewery and Tap, which closed at the turn of the century. Priory House has remained although it has been entirely rebuilt. Despite its humble origins the Bird in Hand has survived the enormous changes made in this section of Newmarket Road. Even modern buildings like the headquarters of the *Cambridge Evening News* have come and gone, replaced by the Cambridge Building Society.

Sun Street, 1901. Sun Street has all but disappeared but local people still use the name. It ran from the corner of Wellington Street to the chapel. By the 1930s there was only one house listed but there was also a Sun Court. As one would expect in Barnwell, the name has its origins in the Sun public house! Built in 1876, the Primitive Tabernacle was inspired by the godless activities of the churchless inhabitants of Barnwell where brothels and breweries were the two biggest industries. Dukes Court was built in 1992 and the Tabernacle may well have inspired its gable ends. Fortunately the church founders didn't live to see what happened to their creation. After closing as a church, the building housed Finbow furniture removers and ended its life as the Carioca night-club. It was wrecked by a fire in 1983.

Sun Street, 1948. This area was transformed by the construction of Elizabeth Way Bridge in 1971 and the redevelopment of individual sites. The humble Bird in Hand has survived the loss of nearly all its neighbours except the car park opposite and the Priory House. Newmarket Road and Barnwell have been transformed from a sleepy pleasant village in the eighteenth century, to the roughest and toughest district of Cambridge in the nineteenth, to one of the meanest and probably dirtiest streets in the twentieth, with brick pits, wood yards, gas and coke works and rubbish pits. But by the beginning of the twenty-first century it was transformed again by retail emporia, offices and gentrified working-class housing.

Cellarer's Chequer, *c.* 1895; Abbey Church, Newmarket Road, *c.* 1865 (above right and below). Barnwell Priory was a large and enormously wealthy institution founded in 1092. Richard II held Parliament there in 1388 and legislated on the homeless! One architectural commentator called the chapel a 'double muddle' as it was a priory not an abbey and was the *capella ante portas* rather than the principal church. The Reformation brought its closure in 1539 and subsequent destruction, although some of the materials were reclaimed for use in Abbey House close by and the new chapel at Corpus Christi College. In the background can be seen the thirteenth-century Cellarer's Chequer which still stands in Beche Road. This is probably misnamed and may have been the prior's personal quarters or a kitchen. Joseph Sturton, who laid out the roads in 1879, decided to sell all the land for speculative building in small plots. The remains of the priory were excavated and even received an entry in the street directories. Today the screen of trees almost hides the church from view but what a tale this building could tell of life on Newmarket Road since the early thirteenth century.

Riverside, 1910, *c.* 1925 and 2002. The chimney of the Cheddars Lane pumping station is now part of a scheduled ancient monument. It has been a dominant feature in the eastern part of Cambridge since it was built in 1894 to pump sewage to the farm at Milton. It was powered by steam generated from burning the town's rubbish. This practice was halted in the Second World War when there was insufficient calorific value as so much was recycled for the war effort. Thereafter, although trade waste was still burnt, household waste went into the brick pits on the other side of Newmarket Road. In 1968 the pumping station was closed but was ultimately saved from demolition by a group of engineering enthusiasts who created the Museum of Technology. The building in front of the chimney is the former engineer's house, next door to the holder of the extensive Gas and Coke Works. The introduction of natural gas brought the end of production in 1969 and gradual redundancy for the remainder of the site. A new Tesco supermarket opened in 2002, and adjacent housing will follow. The two barges *Enid* and *Lizzy* are taking on gas water, the waste product from the manufacture of gas, for transport to King's Lynn. They were the last vestiges of the river traffic that was once the freight artery of Cambridge.

The Leper Chapel, Newmarket Road, in the eighteenth century. The Church of St Mary Magdalene was built as the chapel of the Leper Hospital at Stourbridge, *Stirbitch* or *Stiebrige* in the early twelfth century. In 1211 King John granted the hospital a fair on the vigil and feast of the Holy Cross. By 1279 the hospital owned 24 acres but had ceased to receive lepers despite the opening of the new hospital of St Anthony and St Elegius at the junction of Trumpington Street and Lensfield Road. Stourbridge Fair was of world renown and the church became a sought-after living, often awarded to friends of the bishop. By 1751 it had ceased to be a place of worship and was used for storage for the fair. In 1816 Thomas Kerrich gave the restored chapel to the University, which in turn passed it to the Cambridge Preservation Society in 1951. As with all old ecclesiastical buildings local legend has it that there was a tunnel from here to the Abbey Church or possibly as far as Biggin Abbey. No evidence for such a tunnel was found when the railway was cut through below the level of the chapel. The fair itself lasted until the twentieth century but had faded away by 1932, when only two women and an ice-cream seller turned up to hear the mayor proclaim the fair.

The Globe Inn and former papermills, *c.* 1915. Close examination will reveal some artistic licence in the drawing, which should serve as a caution to those who would use this type of work as an historical source. This ancient site was once the last (or first) habitation for weary travellers to and from Cambridge on the Newmarket Road, which used to turn the corner along what is now Ditton Walk and head for Fen Ditton. It was safer to travel from village to village rather than bypass them with the most direct route. The construction of the turnpike road was itself a sign of safer times. The Globe was a public house for years but has now been divided into three restaurants. The Papermills House is now offices but the mill-race still runs, albeit with reduced force, under the road past the frontage. Papermaking ceased in the early seventeenth century but flour was milled in more recent times. Across the road on the Abbey Stadium site were situated the Papermills tea gardens, the entrance gained under 'a rusty arch of ironwork surmounted by a broken lamp'.

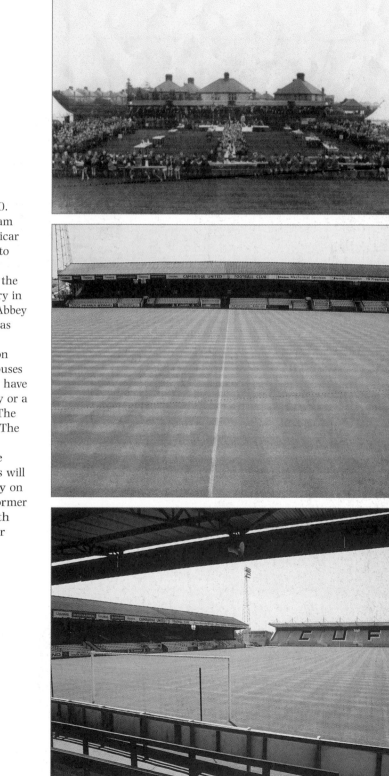

Abbey Stadium, Newmarket Road, *c.* 1950. Cambridge United originated as a local team that was assisted in its formation by the vicar of the Abbey Church in 1912. The move to the current site, which became the Abbey Stadium, was made possible by the gift of the ground by H.C. Francis of the Star Brewery in 1932. Prior to that the club, then called Abbey United, had played on a pitch so poor it was nicknamed the celery trenches. The early photograph shows a substantial celebration under way with the east stand and the houses in Elfleda Road in the background. It may have been a coronation celebration, Labour Day or a feast celebrating the grant of city status. The team became Cambridge United in 1951. The stadium is currently undergoing a transformation with the completion of the south stand as shown; it is hoped that this will be joined by a new north stand built partly on the site cleared by the demolition of the former Corona Works. At the turn of the twentieth century this was the site of Sindall's Power Joinery Mill.

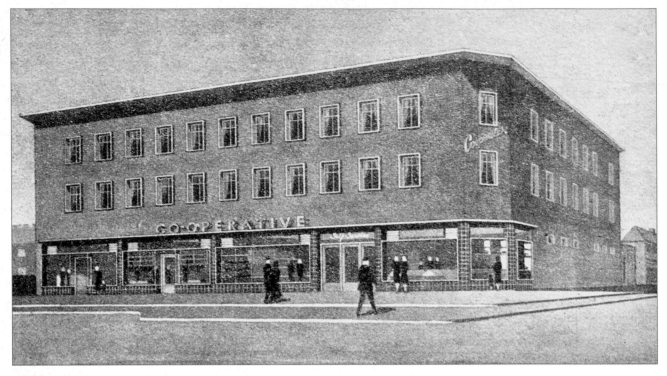

The Co-op, Whitehill Road, *c*. 1965. Until 1936 this was the site of Marshall's first aerodrome. In that year the city bought the former Whitehill Farm although the war interrupted progress on house-building until the early 1950s. The first shops were provided next door in Elfleda Road but they proved inadequate and the Cambridge Co-op built a new style self-service supermarket with flats above. The shop closed in the late 1980s and was converted into its current residential use.

Ivett & Reed, Newmarket Road, *c.* 1905. Cousins Fred Ivett and Sam Reed served together as apprentices at Saint's Monumental Sculptors, next door to Mill Road cemetery. When the owner retired they took over the business and also opened a new shop and stone yard in Newmarket Road, close to the newly created corporation cemetery. Ivett died in 1922 but the firm remains with the Reeds. 'Grandma' Elsie Reed was herself the daughter of a local business family, the Cooks who opened the first petrol garage on Newmarket Road. She was a great fan of Cambridge United. In the late 1940s she founded an over-sixties club which still meets at the community centre today.

The Racehorse, Newmarket Road, *c.* 1985. Built to replace the licensed house at the Airport Hotel in 1964, this was the last public house to remain open in Abbey Ward. It had a colourful history and brawls among its clientele hit the headlines on more than one occasion. With its closure, and the opening of McDonald's restaurant in 2001, a local pub name also disappeared. There was a Racehorse across the railway bridge in the nineteenth century.

Barnwell post office, Newmarket Road, *c.* 1955. Farrance House next door was first occupied by a stonemason who, like Ivett & Reed, needed to be near the new cemetery. In 1938 a small shop was erected alongside, prompted no doubt by the potential trade from the neighbouring factory. For many years it was the only outlet in the immediate area until the council built a parade of shops on Barnwell Road. By 1948 Geoffrey Proctor had taken over the business and the house. His dedicated support for local football earned him the nickname 'Mr Cambridge United' and he served as a director and sometime chairman of the club from 1950 until his death in 1974.

Pye Telecommunications, Newmarket Road, *c.* 1955. First listed as the Home Office ARP stores, local people recall that it was primarily a gas-mask factory. In the postwar period it was taken over by Pye's, once the largest manufacturer of televisions in Britain and a major part of the Cambridge economy. However, the government delay in introducing colour television made the company weak and it was unable to resist the Philips take-over. There followed a steady decline until Philips sold out to Simoco. The Pye name is now lost and the business seems to have disappeared without trace. This building is now the Cambridge Techno-Park, created when the front was replaced with a new façade. The back remained unchanged. It even played a part in the Cambridge Phenomenon (the rapid growth in high technology) by accommodating a department of Acorn Computers.

City cemetery, Newmarket Road, *c.* 1905. The buildings illustrated are the chapel and the superintendent's house. In 1901, as Mill Road neared completion, the council prepared to build a new cemetery outside the town in Fen Ditton. Such was the scale of population growth that the latter was itself a relatively recent construction of 1847, on a site that was then on the edge of the town. Cambridge has continued to grow outwards, particularly after the extension of the boundaries in 1933. Driven by the continued shortage of affordable housing the city has sold the land intended for the cemetery expansion to housing associations and has laid out another new cemetery at the crematorium on the Huntingdon Road, also outside the city – at the moment!

Marshall's New Aerodrome, Newmarket Road, 1929. David Marshall founded the family firm that later became the Marshall Group. His son Arthur enthusiastically took up flying in the 1920s and built an aerodrome at the back of his house, Aviation Hall, on Newmarket Road (far right). Within a few years Cambridge was looking to build new housing to replace the inner-city slums and the City Council reached an agreement to purchase what was Whitehill Farm – Marshall agreed to move further along Newmarket Road. Today Cambridge is still looking to expand further and is planning to move the airport elsewhere to allow for a massive extension to the city.

This 1948 aerial photograph shows the new airport and North Works, the product of rapid wartime growth. In the background is the pre-war Meadowlands estate, with the neighbouring Peverel estate under construction. The newly constructed Barnwell Road was built as part of the 1930s planned ring road. The northern section, intended to cross the Cam at Ditton Meadows, was planned in the 1930s but was postponed as the council then doubted its necessity. In the 1990s furious opposition killed off a revival of the plan despite the completion of the section of Barnwell Road to Coldhams Lane. In the far background the roads for the Whitehill Estate have been laid out, revealing the underlying chalk – and the origins of the ancient name White Hill.

On the Trumpington Road & to Newnham

Old houses in Silver Street, shortly before demolition, *c.* 1890. George Flack was a painter and glazier who lived at no. 2 Newnham, next to Queen's Green on the other side of Silver Street Bridge.

London Road, *c.* 1935. Trumpington lost its village status and parish council in 1934 when it was absorbed into Cambridge. Parts of the village had already been conceded by 1912. Barely one hundred years ago the only public transport to Cambridge was William Haslop's carrier's cart which arrived on Mondays, Wednesdays, Fridays and Saturdays. By the early 1930s Eastern Counties motor omnibuses operated daily but the carrier's cart was still running. Giving the increasing flow of traffic, if this had been an isolated settlement residents would be calling for a bypass. However, it may be a surprise to most to know that before the construction of the Trumpington turnpike road, which operated from 1793 to 1872, the old London road ran to the west of the village centre and church, somewhere in the vicinity of Trumpington Hall.

High Street, *c.* 1905. Unlike Cherry Hinton, which was also absorbed into the city, Trumpington has resisted large-scale housing developments to date and the old High Street has maintained much of its rural character, depite the loss of some buildings.

The war memorial and High Street, Trumpington, *c.* 1925. This area was once called Cross Hill. The lower part of the cross was rediscovered during excavations for the war memorial designed by Eric Gill in 1921. 'Hill' in Cambridgeshire also means a flat open public space, as well as the more traditional definition!

Trumpington Road, at the junction with Latham Road, *c.* 1895. The business of G. Willers, nurseryman, seedsman and florist, operated from this charming house from at least the 1870s until the mid-1930s. It flanks Latham Road, which was named after the Revd Henry Latham, Master of Trinity Hall, who lived at Southacre. The road leads to River Farm and contains some of the finest domestic properties in the city.

Brooklands Avenue, *c.* 1905. Called the Avenue until the 1930s, this tree-lined road was laid out in the mid-Victorian period on the initiative of the Foster family, local bankers, millers and merchants. Richard Foster bought Brooklands Farm from James Burleigh in 1825 and built Brooklands House six years later. Plots were then sold off along the Avenue, aimed at the well-to-do businessmen of the town. Each sale contained a covenant of 1854 limiting the property to residential occupation. It remained a private cul-de-sac with its own gate until public adoption in the late 1920s when a bridge was built over Hobson's Brook to provide a through connection to and from Trumpington Road. At that time it was realised that the elms were diseased and over the years they have been replaced. During the Second World War government offices were 'temporarily' relocated to Brooklands Farm – where they remained for over fifty years! The low-rise buildings will shortly be replaced by new homes 150 years after the Avenue was first laid out for housing. Wymondham House, just visible through the trees, was built as the home of George Kett of Rattee & Kett.

Brookside, 1903, *c.* 1955 and 2002. Brookside was built in the mid- to late nineteenth century with a superb aspect facing Hobson's Brook. The explosion in this type of house building was accelerated by the change in University regulations in 1882 which permitted *all* fellows to marry, rather than restricting such a privilege to those who held particular offices. Barely yards away, however, the Victorians also built the tiny back-to-back houses of Saxon and Gothic Streets, which were to become some of the town's worst slums. Changes in the class structure and social life between the wars and the decline in the requirement for domestic servants through labour-saving devices meant that families no longer needed and could not afford such large properties. Institutions began to occupy the properties as they became available, with the Leys School taking two for their hostels and later sanatorium, followed by the Department of Education, the Botanic Gardens and others. The most famous resident was Henry Fawcett, the blind professor of political economy who served as Postmaster-General and created the parcel post.

Lensfield Road, *c.* 1905. These properties were built as quality housing in the late nineteenth century, but an increasing number were converted for use by medical practitioners. In 1953 there were six dentists, two physicians and one gynaecologist. By the 1970s Downing College, backing on to the site, had taken over two houses for use as student hostels, and this process has accelerated with the construction of accommodation in certain rear gardens. On the opposite side of the road the architect William Wilkins built Lensfield for his own use. In the 1950s this was demolished to make way for the chemistry laboratories.

Trumpington Street, 1872. The Half Moon was demolished in 1875 to make way for Emmanuel Congregational Church. However, it only moved to Little St Mary's Lane. It became a private house in 1915, from which its sign still hangs. Other buildings in the range have survived. In the distance is the ecclesiastical-style tower of the Pitt Building of the University Press, erected in 1831–32 as a monument to William Pitt the Younger. Freshmen have often been fooled into thinking it is a church. The railings on the corner protect the churchyard of Little St Mary's.

Trumpington Street, 1865.

Trumpington Street, 2002. The view through to King's is framed to the right by the fourteenth-century St Botolph's Church, St Botolph being the East Anglian patron saint of travellers and therefore appropriately placed near the Trumpington Gate. Ede & Ravenscroft (left) bought James Neal's academic tailors shop, which dated back to the 1870s. In the distance, partly obscuring King's, stood the Cory building which the owner had refused to sell to the college, thus halting the completion of the Wilkin's Screen (the new street frontage and gatehouse) in 1823. The college finally had its way on the owner's death in 1870 and erected Sir George Scott's Chetwynd Building. Note the advert for bathrooms in the 1865 picture, regarded by some as a luxury facility in college as students were only up for ten weeks at a time!

Trumpington Street, 1862. The property on the left is now Fitzbillies, named after the Museum, which can just be seen in the distance. Beyond is Pembroke College, beholden – like several other colleges – to a female founder, the Countess of Pembroke. What else could a rich woman do with her money but found a college? What she couldn't do was receive a degree – not until 1947! The range and gateway are fourteenth century in origin but were later refaced and the distinctive hexagonal lantern is on the College Chapel which was begun by Wren in 1663. He was the nephew of the Bishop of Ely who gave £5,000 in thanks for his safe release after eighteen years in captivity. In the picture below the fourth house on the right appears to have been rebuilt but with one floor removed. The present open conduit on either side of the street dates from the end of the eighteenth century and replaced an earlier channel that ran down the middle of the road. This is the site of the medieval Trumpington Gate. Across the road ran the King's Ditch, which was so foul that it was also called the Black Ditch.

The Granta Inn, Newnham Mill Pond, 1925. In 1874 this was listed as the Granta Brewery of Bailey & Tebbutt. By the 1920s the Granta operated as a hotel with the Newnham and Queens Garage of Cocks next door. The punt has now replaced the car as one of the foundations of the business.

Newnham Mill, *c.* 1800. The original owner was Count Alan of Brittany, who accompanied William the Conqueror to England in 1066. It was later transferred to the Mortimer family and then to Gonville & Caius College. Queen Elizabeth I once changed horses here on a visit to the town. The Fosters took the tenancy in the nineteenth century but a disastrous fire in 1853 led to a complete reconstruction. The railway arrived in 1845 but the Fosters failed to achieve the construction of a new line and station on Coe Fen and so they closed the mill along with the King's and Bishop's Mills downstream. The mill here later played a small part in the development of scientific instruments, said to be the first Cambridge phenomenon, by housing the London Instrument Company. By 1975 it was a car agents. The building is now restored as the Bella Pasta restaurant and as part of the décor preserves historic features of its industrial past.

Mill Pond, 1900. Newnham Mill had to stop work if the King's and Bishop's Mills blew their horn to signal their right over the water flow. The large malting houses were demolished and rebuilt as houses in yet another road widening scheme. The Jolly Millers, reputedly founded in 1490, was known as the Three Jolly Millers in 1839. It was rebuilt in 1903 and is now in use as a restaurant.

Newnham Road, 1925. The 'bypass road' indicated by the sign was Fen Causeway, which was constructed in 1928 by widening Coe Fen Lane and building a bridge and a new road across Sheep's Green as a work scheme for the unemployed. The Caius Perse Almshouses were built here in 1886, having originally stood in Free School Lane near the original Perse School. Next door were the Newnham Schools, replaced today by the Shell Garage. In the Middle Ages flooding could cut Newnham off from Cambridge. With the current and predicted growth in traffic, residents may well not object if it happens again.

Grantchester Street, *c.* 1920. This is the entrance to a pleasant suburban cul-de-sac of early 1920s and 1930s housing known as Newnham Croft. The name pre-dates the modern estate – Newnham was a Saxon settlement, a daughter hamlet to neighbouring Grantchester. To the left the Granta Housing Society has built on the former University hockey ground. On the right is Newnham Co-op, the no. 7 branch.

Eltisley Avenue, *c.* 1920, 1925 and 2002, showing all too clearly the onward march of pre-war suburbia. The stark newness of the terraces is in contrast to the current view, tempered by vegetation. Little else has changed apart from the proliferation of the motor car. The local greengrocers have survived but no longer advertise British wines or English and Foreign Fruit and Veg! The early residents included a commercial traveller, clerks, a college groundsman, gardeners, a clothier, a motor engineer and a hotel manager.

From Magdalene Bridge along the Chesterton Road

View from Castle Hill, 1838. The distinctive houses in the foreground still stand in Chesterton Lane. In the middle distance can be seen Jesus Lock. Chesterton resembles a disjointed settlement isolated from Cambridge by the river and the large tracts of common up to Maid's Causeway. There is no visible route through to Chesterton village. Foot travellers used the ferries to cross the river and vehicles joined the Ely turnpike further to the west. Chesterton Road was laid out in the late nineteenth century to facilitate housing developments.

Magdalene Bridge, *c.* 1885. It is sometimes called the Great Bridge in contrast to the Small Bridges at Newnham. No Cambridge foundry was large enough to cast the span so only the railings were made at Charles Finch's foundry in Bridge Street in 1823. Magdalene Bridge carried traffic through the city as the A604 until the northern bypass, now the A14, opened in 1980. The bridge was refurbished in 1983 but then was largely closed to through traffic in 1999.

Magdalene Street, 1870. The Pickerel, meaning young pike, is an early sixteenth-century inn with a nineteenth-century frontage. In 1873 Magdalene College demolished the buildings in the right foreground that contained Kimbolton and Salmon Lanes, the latter accessed through a Gothic archway. The range to the left survived Magdalene's ambitious expansion plans from the early twentieth century, thus preserving the best collection of buildings of this period in the city. The demise of river freight moved the economic focus of the town away to the railway and brought about the stagnation of river properties, thus preserving them from redevelopment. Magdalene Street was also fortunate to survive a particularly insensitive road widening scheme that would have resulted in its complete destruction.

Chesterton Lane and Magdalene Street, 1911. This range was removed in 1912 to extend Magdalene College grounds. In 2001 workers excavating foundations for Anglian Water's new sewers discovered only the second medieval hoard found in Cambridge. The box fell apart on removal but it contained about 1,800 coins with a face value of about £10. Hidden at around the time of the Black Death they represented about three or four years' wages for the average craftsman. Saddler Alfred Bennett and cab driver Albert Pointer were the last occupants of the property: one wonders what they would have thought if they had known that they were so close to such riches.

Chesterton Lane, *c.* 1905. Traffic again brought changes to this junction as the timber yards next to the Folk Museum were removed to widen Northampton Street. The houses in Northampton Street remain as student accommodation, facing inwards to the college rather than out to the street and creating a somewhat dead frontage. Further road widening took a section of St Giles' churchyard. This was the site of the first traffic lights in Cambridge.

The county gaol, *c.* 1885, and Shire Hall, 2002. The first stone of the gaol was laid in 1802. It was said to have come from the foundations of the old castle, the stone from which had been carted away by Cambridge colleges and enterprising citizenry until only the Gatehouse remained. In 1891 there were eighty-four inmates in what was known as the House of Correction. Prisoners also came from Huntingdon, Hertfordshire, Suffolk and Essex. The gaol closed in 1916 and local researchers may care to note that it served as the local record office in 1922. In 1930 over eight thousand people toured the building before it was demolished to make way for the new Shire Hall, which used some of the cast-off bricks. No doubt some of those bricks also ended up in Cambridge homes!

Arundel House Hotel, Chesterton Road, *c.* 1905. Built from around 1880, the somewhat grand Sentis Terrace has almost all been converted into the Arundel House Hotel. In 1970 Major Norfolk left Pye to purchase 61 Chesterton Road and opened the hotel with just twelve bedrooms. It has grown incrementally across the terrace and now occupies eight of the nine houses and offers 105 rooms. The former coach-house and Frost's Garage at the rear have been converted from their original industrial use. The first fee-paying horse-omnibuses began operating from the latter in 1894, although they only lasted ten years. In 1999 restoration of the hotel's exterior was begun.

Chesterton Road and Jesus Lock, 1886.

Opposite: Chesterton Road and Jesus Lock, 1887. The boat trip was part of an inspection of the river by the Conservators of the Cam, the authority responsible for managing the river between the King's Mill and Clayhithe. On the road can be seen the delivery vehicle of Robert Sayle & Co. The bank opposite was landscaped and planted with trees and renamed the Victoria Great (Diamond) Jubilee Memorial Pleasure Ground. Behind the houses are the Alexandra Gardens, on the site of a former brick pit. Trees now obscure most of the buildings except Henry Giles House on the right, containing the Job Centre. It was completed by Horace Darwin's Cambridge Scientific Instrument Company in 1961. Until then the company had used the original house seen at the top of the page, having built a factory to the rear in 1913. The terrace now occupied by the Arundel Hotel had yet to be completed in 1887.

Jesus Lock, 1880. The lock replaced an earlier system that had been installed at the Fort St George further downstream. The footbridge was built in about 1851 and had a low-level crossing over the weir with a 'cock-up' bridge over the lock. In 1890 another storey was built on to the lock-keeper's cottage and in 1892 the footbridge was condemned and replaced with a level structure from the Chesterton Bank.

River views, 1815, 1842 and 2002. Looking upstream towards Thompson's Lane, such long-distance views are not possible today because of the mass of trees obscuring the sightlines. The two upper pictures were drawn when the river trade was at its height. The year 1845 saw the advent of the railway and the river folk's world came crashing down.

Chesterton Road and Victoria Road, *c.* 1905. At the far end of Victoria Road is St Luke's Church, completed in 1886 and able to seat 776. Chesterton was enclosed in 1838 but the two largest land-owners were not disposed towards housing developments so initial growth was patchy. Scales Hotel had a distinguished entrance but little else of any note and was later replaced by the Portland Arms. The Great Eastern Railway operated its parcels office from one part of the hotel. The buildings on the right of Victoria Road remain, except for Dant's bakery shop, but they are now hidden by the trees.

Chesterton Road, *c.* 1920. To the right is a Shell garage which only closed a few years ago. On the central island is Lloyds Bank, built in the typical style of the 1920s and 1930s. In front of the bank is a dog water trough presented to Cambridge by Prince Chula-Chahta-Bonse to commemorate his dog Toby, who died while the prince was up at Trinity in the 1930s. On the left is the Tivoli, which was opened in 1925 and replaced the Spring Brewery. It closed in 1956 and since then has had a varied career but survives as a public house. To the far left can be glimpsed the entrance to the underground toilets.

Chesterton Road, *c.* 1925. A death knell seemed to be sounded for the large terrace houses when they became a central traffic island in the 'gyratory' traffic management system for what is colloquially known as 'Mitcham's Corner'. Further relief came with the opening of Elizabeth Way in 1971. These former townhouses were converted to bed-sits and recent refurbishments have led to the creation of some quality flats. At the end of the terrace were the offices of the Urban District Council, later replaced by a police box. The UDC had twelve members, who met on the first Wednesday in the month. The Chesterton Rural District Council met on Thursdays at the Workhouse!

Chesterton Road, *c.* 1925 and 1930. When James Mitcham, family butcher, let his son Charles build his drapery shop on the garden of the family home in 1909 he could never have guessed that his name would become synonymous with the corner of Chesterton Road and Victoria Avenue long after the business had closed. Charles Mitcham wryly admitted that he made his own niche in the market more by accident than by design as he made a mistake in estimating the profit margins rather than undercutting the competition. But his talent for advertising – note the brash roof-mounted signboard for his sale at Mitcham's Corner – helped his business to become a great success and he made this part of Chesterton his own. He sold the business after the Second World War but the name was retained for some years. Even when the name was changed and the signboard came down the legend continued and when the new road system was created in 1967 it was labelled the Mitcham's Corner roundabout. Definitely worthy of a blue plaque!

Victoria Avenue, 1890. Chesterton has a long history as an independent settlement but with the growth of the town in the second part of the nineteenth century the pressure grew for its amalgamation into 'Greater Cambridge'. Before 1850 the Jolly Waterman was said to be the only building between Chesterton and Cambridge. In 1890 Victoria Avenue and Bridge were constructed partly to persuade Chesterton that it should merge with Cambridge. Provision was made for a second bridge but this was not carried through until Elizabeth Way was opened in 1971! The Urban District Council held out until 1912, when the boundary extension extinguished Chesterton's independence. The Jolly Waterman was merely a beerhouse for many years but its corner position in the heart of what had become a local shopping centre encouraged the brewery to rebuild it as a public house.

Ferry path, *c.* 1925. Townsend's moved to Chesterton in 1989 after taking over the cycle shop of W. Ison but they have kept the name to operate their wholesale business. Formed as the Light Blue Cycle Company in 1895 in Norfolk Street, they have painted their building in their traditional colour, light blue.

Chesterton Road and Hall, 1950. This Jacobean brick mansion was built in the second quarter of the seventeenth century with subsequent adaptations and extensions including an octagonal tower. It was bought in 1971, at the time of the creation of Elizabeth Way, formerly Haig Road, since when it has been converted into City Council flats. The road scheme divorced the hall from its garden and coach-house, which are now on the other side of the large roundabout.

Chesterton Tower, 1850, *c.* 1935 and 2002. Six hundred years ago a grateful Henry III gave Chesterton Church to Cardinal Gualo, the Papal Legate, for his part in keeping the peace, and the cardinal duly bestowed it on his foundation of the Abbey of Vercelli in Italy. The tower was built in the mid-fourteenth century and has a ground floor reception hall that was probably used by the representative of the Abbey. Reclaimed by Henry VI in 1444 it later came into the possession of Trinity College. Sometimes known as the old Abbey, the 1850 drawing shows it in use as a barn. Restored in 1949, it now serves as offices with flats built in the grounds. It is a complete unit rather than a fragment and is a rare example of a dwelling appropriated for the representative of a foreign power.

The Green Dragon, Water Street, *c.* 1885, *c.* 1925 and 2002. The Horse Grind and Ferry carried horse-drawn vehicles as well as foot passengers. It was made obsolete by the construction of the footbridge in 1935. All five ferries along the river were eventually made redundant through the provision of road and foot crossings. The last to go was at Elizabeth Way and it was used by the builders constructing the bridge. The Green Dragon is part of a fine timber-framed range and well worth a visit. And as this journey around Cambridge comes to an end why not step inside and enjoy a pint?

Acknowledgements & Picture Credits

All the modern photographs are by Tony Jedrej. Unless otherwise stated all the old photographs are from the Cambridgeshire Collection, Cambridgeshire County Council, with the exception of: page 20, St John's Chapel, by kind permission of Mr Douglas E. Daniels from the Victorian photographers' catalogue from the stationery shop of Edwin Doo; page 65, The Red Lion, by kind permission of the Cambridge Antiquarian Society; pages 68 and 82, Cherry Hinton Hall and The Racehorse from a private collection; page 77, The Leper Chapel, by kind permission of the Master & Fellows of Downing College; page 79, Abbey Stadium *c.* 1950, by kind permission of Brian Attmore and Graham Nurse from their book *Cambridge United Football Club*; and page 125, *The Bumps*, by permission of Cambridge City Council.

My special thanks go to the staff of the Cambridgeshire Collection, without whose patience, help and support this book would not have been possible, with special mention for Chris Jakes and the team – Ann Asher, Sabine Bajahr, Fiona Parish and Sue Slack; to the trustees, staff and residents of Newmarket Open Door, who permitted me time to complete this work at a difficult period; to my colleagues and the staff of Cambridge City and County Councils, whose collective enthusiasm for their work is always worth commendation and goes further than they know; and once again to all those who research, write and donate items to libraries and archives without whom none of this would be possible or worthwhile.

The Bumps, Fen Ditton, by Percy Robert Craft, *c.* 1905. No river visit should close without some mention of rowing. The social event was as important as the sport. For many years this picture was displayed in the Lending Library but when the library moved to new premises it was put into storage. After restoration it was recently returned to the same building, now the Tourist Office.